Mr. McDoogle's Farm

Written and Illustrated By:
Marie Whitton

For My Husband
Greg

For My Children
Gregory, Ann-Marie &
Kimberly

For My
Grandchildren

On this farm -
are there any secrets in store?
Will visiting be a bore?
Everything looks so quiet and still,
Life on a farm has no frill.
Come on in - let's see,
What there will be.

Farmer McDoogle -
"Welcome to my farm",
"It has a lot of charm".
"Tomorrow - will be a busy day",
"Come and learn how to run
my farm my way".

Over the horizon -the rising of the sun,
Work – it is a ton.
So early and bright.
What a wonderful sight.
The rooster would crow – Cock-A-Doodle-Doo,
To which – the cows would reply – Moo.
It's time for us to rise and shine,
Without a whine.

For the horses - it is time to feed,
This is Mr. McDoogle's deed.
They like oats and hay,
This is what they eat every day.

To the field - the cows will go out,
There is no doubt.
All day,
They will eat hay.
Even the bull,
Will eat until he is full.

Chickens and chicks are hungry for corn,
Mr. McDoogle will feed in the morn.
The rooster will watch over his flock,
All around the clock.

Let's look in on the hens,
We are counting eggs by the tens.
Collecting some of the eggs -
Mr. McDoogle will,
This is his morning drill.
Letting the other eggs hatch,
The chicks - he will catch.

Next, Mr. McDoogle will feed the hogs.
Where are they? In the Bog?
In the mud - they are going to play,
All day - there they will stay.

Mr. McDoogle gets water from the well,
It is time to ring the bell.
Farm animals hear the sound,
They come running from all around.

Mr. McDoogle will blow his horn,
It is time to harvest the corn.
To market - the corn he will take.
Corn bread the baker will bake.

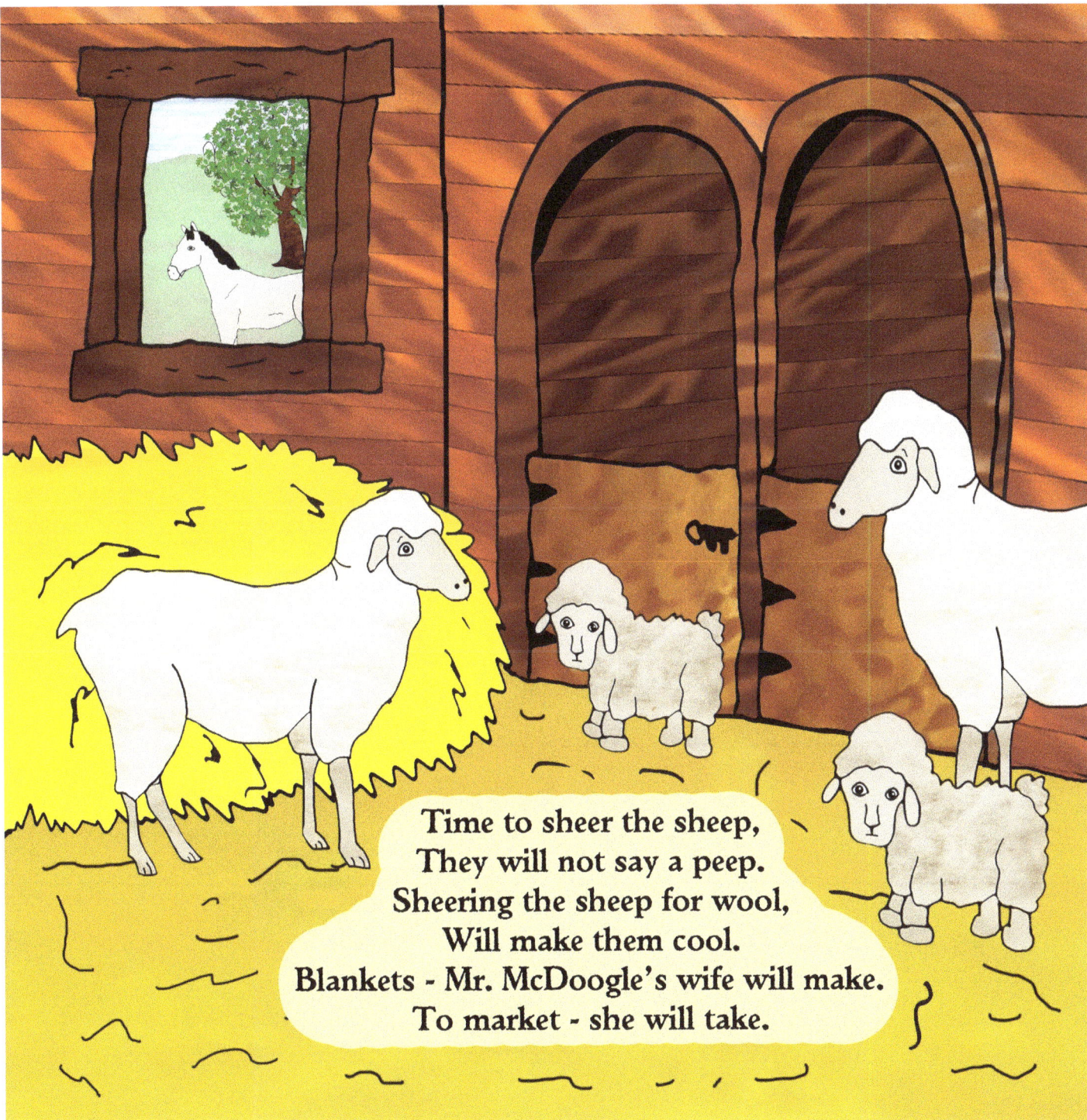

Time to sheer the sheep,
They will not say a peep.
Sheering the sheep for wool,
Will make them cool.
Blankets - Mr. McDoogle's wife will make.
To market - she will take.

"Thank you for coming", Mr McDoogle
did say.
We certainly had a wonderful day.
Come back to see us next year,
I will still be here.

www.ingramcontent.com/pod-product-compliance
Lightning Source LLC
Chambersburg PA
CBHW060754150426
42811CB00058B/1409

* 9 7 8 0 5 7 8 4 7 7 7 3 2 *